Soggy Socks *and* Shoes

Charles Williams

NEWMAN SPRINGS PUBLISHING
320 Broad Street
Red Bank, NJ 07701

First originally published by Newman Springs Publishing 2018

ISBN 978-1-64096-370-2 (Paperback)
ISBN 978-1-64096-371-9 (Digital)

Printed in the United States of America

America

Dialect is complex since anit is in the dictionary
Tee shirts hold impression
Miles of thought in sound and space
Segregation, daring signs
Equality
3/5ths Agreement, Emancipation Proclamation, Affirmative Action
Earn those reparations
Soul Train reflections, sexual expression
(connection for the funk)

Jackie Robinson, humility and heart break
Freedom Riders
Ballot or the bullet
Choke, now and then
Swallow, overcome
Bessie coming years
America love it or leave it
Presidential reply
I'm black and I'm proud
Bills become Laws. Is Civil Rights a white lie?

Acid jazz
Planetary echoes
Justice
Supreme Court response
Soul channel
Cuddle up, smile
Free at last
spell the message
Keep your eyes on the prize.
Opportunity, separate but equal
I hold no ill regards
Guess who's coming to dinner?
America!

One-n-Three

think about it
diagnosed with cancer
challenges of illness
immunotherapy
radiotherapy
chemotherapy
surgery
hospice
paid for by Medicare

Quality of Life Crimes

question of assumption
voice of a citizen
scream were no one is
safe isolation
go where silence is
free to question government
over criminalized

Increasing

....

currently shopping
best value
consider
select group opportunity
think
specialize goods
satisfaction don't wait
sooner chance
exceptional service
earned

Old Hickory Knew Her, Well?

Davy Crockett and Sam Houston died at the Alamo.
It took a nation of millions to hold her away from her slaves.
To her Buffalo Soldiers were a slap in the face
Nervous and trembling
Generations have never left the Tomilson plantation
What can the righteous do?
Share crop and repopulate
Notice the ideology of Jefferson Davis
The Confederate States of Americas
Texas!

Kwanzaa 2.0

One hundred forty million
The African Diaspora
living in life
striving in business
you are invited
taste the libation
Argentina, Barbados, Brazil, Canada, Colombia, Cuba,
Dominican Republic, Ecuador, France, Guyana, Germany,
Grenada, Haiti, Italy, Jamaica, Mexico, Peru, Puerto Rico,
Spain, Suriname, Trinidad and Tobago, United Kingdom,
United States,
Venezuela
to build the African Union
Harumbee

Da Moment

We Pray
Dear God,

We still praying
asking for spare change to feed a habit
looking ran over in a movement of Civil Rights
marching on with concern of how to get you to buy
Songs, dances, interest

What have you to do
flush
Greed, Hate, Stereotypes, Lust
we are equal
The Golden Rule
potential

United We Stand
nicely designed with divinity
the moment you can admit
There is room for revitalization
Outreach

Da moment tolerance absorbs pain of compromise

Body Movement

See what motivated that action
personality
a reaction
patience grows power
achievement
great results
Did you want that to happen?
Reflex might of thoughts, ideas, belief, and grasp

Women's Day

Yeah, Critical Protocol for a world that greaves with pain
With you is where I want to be

God is worthy of praise
Feminine mystic engulf the most high
with music and lecture and prayer
Let us understand life lead through ancient scriptures

I find it fascinating how the physical is nothing
The world didn't give it to me
And where were you?
He carried me

The cross
Where he died for our sins on Calvary

"Let the church say"
And here our heart ache and pain
Yes, you should remember me from Sunkist beach
Summer set in fold out chair
Perfume fragrance the air

Soon to be in heaven
say no fool
That's great getting up morning?
there's a train leaving soon
my savior (for me)
Lord, I am on my way

Sneaky Sensation

dress code
loosen up
Treat your dogs
stroll with high-end high-tops
against gravity
icon sneaker
lizard lace-ups
blitz your toes
peppermint extract
feet-quenching
smooth operators

Viewing

entertainment experience
you can be killed for a steak dinner, few dollars, and a pint of Hennessy
pay less, options for twelve months
premium channels, installation, and technical support
High Definition free for life
avoid family conflicts
watch TV on your smart phone or tablet

Criminal Justice Reform

issues of flaws are issues of people
costing taxpayers' money
disenfranchising people
creating economic disorder
increasing crime
decreasing the quality of life and education
appeal to convicted felons

Your Fault

can't make work
pay
build a life
tolerable
stable
can't save short and long term
Living hand to mouth
Lazy!

Mobile Register

Africa Town
package stores and super markets
from the Gulf of Mexico
free of hatred and terror
home of "Mardi Gras"
to the ends of Antarctica
sin was not invented
darling words
inevitable
What is the stars?
Obey laws
flash affair it was . . .
same-sex marriage licenses
need a receipt

hard hat area
paisley and feathers
combination
black on purple text
red on yellow text
leopard and checkered
combination
To be continued

Money-saving

friendly and experienced
you can count on
day or night
get on
reasons
sense to inquire
attainable soundness
claims-paying

or even on a Saturday night

all kinds end
Forty-sixth street pharmacy in Times Square
What a joint! Forget it.
Who you'd meet?
Frolicked
right thigh

Notice

....

Unfortunately
means coverage
You want to continue being a customer?
Payment or Cancellation
received or post marked
online or over the phone
reach out
attention matters
Confirmation is recognized.

Dare to Be Different

....

peer pressure point
re-imagines
take action
self-help life
tackle a problem
have your own reasons
choose inaction
if they want it
benefit

Innovators

....

winning personality
concentration and focus
self-identify
professional life
pitching investors
authority through collaboration
risk-prone behavior

Halt or Help

bright and bubbly
judgment day
everyone calling you captain
incandescent
carbonated soda
wig-wag high beam lights
versatile personality
"pursuit-rated"
kill switches
agile interceptor
prime time
armed with facts
bonding time devour funds

Purpose

best leadership
move and humble
inspire and create
believe in change
blaze new trails
singular vision and course
not bossing
fearlessness, clarity, and courageous

Fear Society

you have a right to be offended
Freedom of expression
she feared to tell him the truth
thick-skinned
Western society
diversify
the pen became my tears
illegal if insight violence
(classless)
fashionable

Refrigeonomics

identifies an economic class or world rate of country
consumer evolution
too rich to die
economic growth
Solar power refrigerator
keep it fresh
farm field to the market (three times a day)
cost of living
Do you know what you will eat in the future?
Small percent of energy is used for cooling food in the U.S.A.
reflections refrigeration
I have beer!

Options

....

love offering
no-cost
part of many being
payment
seven days a week
respond by enrollment
participation needed
clinical supervision
travel provided
working with others

Drones

once upon a time we were colored
before then Negros
the Butler did it
clue
twelve years a slave
costumes for sale
the Help
cross colors
electronic frontier or freedom foundation
maintain peaceful efforts

Happy Daze

holiday stress
extra dollars
all you need
get you by
check until
bank statement
money for today
lunch for two
gift basket
dinner for two
$100 cash

Memory of Gardens

portfolio package
convenient owning
affordably
permanent records
how-and where-memorialized
people cry for me
impact of bereavement
cemetery space
life ends

Guest

....

you water
who does that
it's still blocking off the session
I'll just be quiet
go to print
sausage and egg biscuits $3.50
feminine mystic alerts attention

The Inequality Hoax

home of veterans
lose conciseness
hyper segregation with retaining wall
property value
public housing stock
mass incarceration of the poor
policy of plans
risk of results
reparations
Federal housing segregated

Retirement Liabilities

behind the Cori numbers
Don't sit back
cost of living stops when you die
same depression in rates cost of funding
That's a big omission
liability is big
prices of zeros go up
But if you are now sixty?

Labor

....

automated intensive technology
Can't make the grade.
(million dollars were are you)
Try to think better job more money
job of figuring out what you want
Only time will tell
trying to get my baby back to me
The job of getting more?

Slack

....

progress seems pleasant
Beer want taste romantic?
No shame in being a boss
philosophy meeting someone the sky is blue and I love you
things take time
socially look like flaunting or bragging
grandfathers before time has changed
less humble decision
same routine
proud of earned success

Southern Literature

yes I
my African American experience
captured by a region
folk, y'all, nigger
tradition
heritage

Inserting

I have life
not a boy
Man, kind to those kind to me
questions of my personality
need not an answer from me
Authority
you have none
interest you posses
wonder all you want
I choose not to address

Social Skills

well rested
mandatory meeting
are you settled
job adjustment
breakfast sectional
work day commute
good morning, good afternoon, good evening
rely on team work
being a benefit to others

Lane

....

break through
work all day and night
24/7 . . . 365
never stop to wonder
never give up aspirations
what you have is yours
some envy joy and salvation
many lust companionship
peace of mind devalued
legs spread apart
stretching
running
driving

Memories

personal view
How was it?
Chance of recollections
embedded in the mind

Forward

....

Thy will be done
though I become scorned
no mask, or smile
choice to survive
my name, my number
in prison or society
civilization under breath
old days, same beliefs
change never comes
appreciation never endured
tolerance of personality and desire to inspire

Permission

Do you love?
If so opportunity
specialize in matching people
study-related
currently conducted
volunteers may receive
medication (in the area)
simply toll-free
convenient visit
duration investigation
compensation cover time
multiple amounts
connection
future interest and third parties
sell, rent, or share
publicly based on general demographics

Yours

....

message to your plan
put rules in play
phone on
customer
It's easy!
Time just
enter give
Don't panic.
Account funds
select directly
secure immediately

Reward

for value
That's it!

Demanding Business

chat of risk
fascinating, never
will trying people
users can't do it all
your enterprise
sale controversy
can sales force?
Effortlessly run on premises
most-deserving clientele

Robert E. Lee

I guess you knew "The Black History of the White House."
Nigger is in the dictionary
You could "not turn your sword against Virginia"
heritage of The Civil War
hatred of paying African Americans to work
The Confederacy salutes Robert E. Lee still today
a slave having knowledge of self, would disturb you?
Ku Klux Klan
Jim Crow Laws
ways of Jefferson Davis
Robert E. Lee implemented
"The Objectification of the African American Experience."

Pronunciation

it had to breath
day-to day
get informed
light shimmer
old school or old age
time caught you confused
brave relief
Now! You know how to spell.
Extras
stimulate conversation
grant mercy to those listeners

Nobody

....

who you know,
what you accomplish,
when you do something,
where your life go,
why you got kids.
Now deal with it?

Deeds

....

American idea
acres and taxes
community outreach
gambling on tomorrow
appreciate value

Lazy

body of dust will
opinion stimulate brain
go through with voice
comfort calms nerves
time calculate effort
notice, note, and neglect

Global 2000

exciting and helpful
Are you satisfied with your present circumstances?
Unique insight
real workings of the financial world
delighted you decided
changes on the portion
tax tricks
retirement funds and real estate
combined, expanded, and premium
throughout the year you'll enjoy

Drifting Derelict

no regret, no get it
mind-boggling
drove his obsession
trash-strewn repositories
then as the sin
worth the hassle
who may have been?
Cannot comprehend
skin game

Day-to-Day

so hold the release date
in or on
respective fields
attitudes change
Brand Ambassador
how does it feel?
Striving for success
unwanted interest
definitely tingly
to warm the winter
in those shoes
come Groundhog Day
biblical power
sacred to me
recognize the Creator
feeding on the energy
sending out shock waves
common center each and off other's
every day

Analytic Services

....

and we maintain safeguards to protect you
personal information
to improve services
during transactions
live better
reporting
current and former
for verification
need-to-know basis

Contemplation of Morality

attractive figure
to see what is today
Cloths to wash. Mouths to feed!
La, La
children
money well spent
all you want
Need
fix your life

Love of Sex

deflection of the train
Sex drives today dreams
times ruff
put on
show out
Interaction
Intercourse

multiple erections
Pleasure
sin is sensation
Marriage your commitment
walking dreaming of sex

Wash Your Face Mr. Morning Man

Objectionable ideas are universal
every penny you got?
Observe and know
apprehend
opportunity
at home by the fire
Ready
Underneath noise
makes life possible
possessed by a vision
embrace sublime reality
disrupt and destroy oppression

Now We Must Choose!

Responsibility
expression
visibility
perception
attention to detail
relations
Unity
security
privacy
Assets
now you must choose your future

Breadcrumbs

....

Personnel wealth
cheaper to absorb the loss
plan to pay
do not stack
awareness is keen
this is unsafe
service area
Phone rings unanswered
Climate Change
flipping the planet earth
savings earn appreciation
people part ways
Moral strength of will
so fly

Love Those That Love You

uncomfortable
chilling silence
I want needs met
you rent
tired of not having
Everything is expensive
what to own
part of a team
Reliability
beyond will power

Thirty Years or Less

How many kids you got?
Dreamer
smoke the mistletoe
everyday celebration
fornication
give yourself a chance
Selfishness
career opportunistic
earned income and debt relief
the club
the corner
guys flock
will you respect me in the morning . . .
What's it look like?

Real Foresight

accomplishments necessary
recognize the piece
roll you over
no re-sequenced phrases
myself machine presented
Nocturnal
fatty foods you consume
dwelling chaotic
lommite dust coated

Hat Trick

still fair
one hundred feet of here
at the top of your screen
watching
distance or high
time reel
ahead you can vote
cost of a ballot ire
Popularity
meanwhile
on net, on the money
hard-work
conquer the cold
bring it off
gem play

Power to the State!

You can leave
sickness and health benefits
Blessed to have a job with flexibility.
Security of payment
muckraking
freedom to earn more
fresh air
liability a privilege
submit to education
certification in the state of . . .

Notify

forward goal
Could today guarantee promise deserved?
Avoid charges
account debt
creditor responsibility
honored
extended terms and conditions
reply evaluating the future
reviewing purpose
request furnished
applicable law result
correspondence
signing disclosures
device expressly message
automatic consent

Question
....

Why are earthquakes not weather?
The most powerful thing on earth
nature going nuts
amazing
electro static field
violent chain reaction
Planetary motion
Plate Tectonics
shift
not descending
ascending . . .

Let Me Know If It's Real

marching
yacky, yacky
Emotional formation
hype
Life is too short to wait till the next day.
What is it about?
Moving money with a plan.
More interest
assets obtained
knowledge gained

Sold Aluminum

to do better
cold life
It ain't easy being me
try
losses enable prosperity
get that paper
do you know who to trust?
Making money
scheme and plot
what became of you?

The Dating Game

Call the police, criminal trespass
Domestic violence
Love under a microscope
Enchantment of happiness
infatuation will occur
conversation we bolster of achievements
making it perfect for each other
friend
Just want to know?
Discounted reality

Present to Win

Take time keep on moving
8:00 hit the job
On some long term stability
it will happen?
money
get up at 5:00 eat
Meditate commute to work
Often punctual
exclusive luxury

Inside

New, we all know
resolutions
list them, keep them
fortunately
easy going
no obligation
525,600 minutes in a year
time to save money
subsequent occurrences
details and amounts
fit your needs
satisfaction of economic freedom

Fraud Liability

annual purchases
transfer cash
transaction
overdraft protection
calculate balance
change terms and residents
penalty
paying consumer finance
after that variable APR
benefits online
no fee offered
balance transfers three percent
Sincerely

Living is No Laughing Matter

Glorified duty
referral
point
Donate
time
management
Self-check
gift
card
media
public
notice
tracking individuals
freedom
democracy
Resolve

CPSIA information can be obtained
at www.ICGtesting.com
Printed in the USA
LVHW032033021118
595813LV00001B/23